INDEX

Page 2 - Heidi's introduction.
Page 4 - Heidi's poem.
Pages 5-34 - Jokes.
Pages 35-40 - What do you call a...jokes.
Pages 41-50 - One liner jokes.
Pages 51-55 - Celebrity jokes.
Pages 56-61 - Riddles.
Pages 61-63 - Friend's jokes.
Pages 64-68 - Fun facts.
Pages 69-70 - Riddle answers.
Page 71 - Dedication

Hello, I'm Heidi and I'm ten years old.
I am raising money for Alzheimer's Research UK to help my Great Uncle Ian and people like him who are living with Alzheimer's.
I have been raising money for Alzheimer's Research UK since 2021 when my first challenge was a 603 mile walk, Land's End to John 'O Groats which raised over £16,500.00. My second challenge started in 2023, a 214 mile bike ride from Paris to London, which raised over £7,000.00.
I have now finished my third challenge which was to use Heidi Power, cycling, walking, swimming, scooting, even a pedalo to travel the 215 miles between the 12 teams stadia who founded the football league in 1888.
I am hoping that the money raised from this book will help to find a cure for Alzheimer's.
I love jokes, riddles, puzzles and fun facts and I wanted to share some with you.
Thank you for buying my book.
From Heidi X

My Dad manages my social media and if you want to follow my adventures then I'm on X @fundraiserheidi

Almost one million people are living with dementia today.
Tragically, not one of them will survive.
Alzheimer's Research UK exists to change that.
As the UK's leading dementia research charity, the team are working to revolutionise the way dementia is treated, diagnosed and prevented.
And then, Alzheimer's Research UK will find a way to cure it.
To do this, the charity is investing in the best research, powering the most forward-thinking scientists and joining forces with world-class organisations.
With the help of their supporters, like me, the charity will not stop until dementia can no longer destroy lives.
Alzheimer's Research UK exists for a cure.

This poem was written by Heidi in her back garden when she was seven.
Such wise words from someone so young…

ODD
It's okay to be odd, to be different.
It's fine when you can't find something.
It's okay when you have to buy something again.
It's okay to not be perfect.
It's okay to have an illness.
It's okay to not be able to cook, ride a bike, stand up, put clothes on or drive.
It's okay to not have hair.
It's okay to be a nerd.
It's okay to be white, brown or black.
It's okay to not have legs.
It's okay to only have half an arm.
It's okay to have a lot of pets.
It's okay to not have any pets.
It's okay to like superheroes or history.
It's okay to not have friends.
It's okay to not always be happy.
It's okay to show your feelings.
It's okay to wear a wig.
It's okay to be you.

JOKES...

Made up by Heidi Barker:
What is a cat's favourite Ed Sheeran song?
Purrrrrfect.

Made up by Heidi Barker:
Why do firefighters slide down poles?
Because they can't slide up them.

Made up by Heidi Barker:
What does a dog want for christmas?
A mobile bone.

Made up by Heidi Barker:
Lilo had to go to hospital because she had a cut on her head. The doctor gave her a Stitch.

Why did the student eat his homework?
Because it was a piece of cake.

Why did the elephant cross the road?
Because it was the chicken's day off.

My girlfriend kept complaining that I was always acting like a detective, she said we should split up so I said "that's a good idea, we'll cover more ground that way".

If you're American when you go into the bathroom and Australian when you come out, what are you when you're in there?
European.

What did the fish say when he swam into a wall?
Dam.

How do the oceans say hello to each other?
They wave.

What do you call a detective alligator wearing a vest?
An investigator.

What's blue and smells like paint?
Blue paint.

How do you know if there's an elephant in your fridge?
Because the door won't shut.

Why did the banana go to the doctors?
It wasn't peeling very well.

Did you know that diarrhoea is hereditary?
It runs in your jeans.

My wife said "Do you know, I think you love that silly football team more than you love me. What would you do if you had to choose, Me or West Brom?"
I miss her sometimes.

What's E.T. short for?
Because he's got little legs.

Why are pirates called pirates?
Because they arrrrrrr.

Why did the baker have smelly hands?
Because he kneaded a poo.

What's a horse's favourite TV show?
Neigh-bours.

What did the cheese say when it saw itself in the mirror?
Hallou-mi.

Someone has stolen all of the inflatables from the local swimming pool. They haven't caught the suspect yet. I reckon they've decided to lilo.

Spider knocked for his friend millipede and asked if he was coming out to play. Millipede said "yes" and spider went outside to wait for him. An hour later millipede still hadn't come outside. So spider went back in and asked what the delay was. Millipede said "I'm just putting my shoes on"

Why couldn't the bike stand up on its own?
Because it was two tyred.

What is a pirate's favourite shop?
Aaarrrrrrgos.

What's the difference between an Indian and an African elephant?
One's an elephant.

What's the difference between being an angry circus owner and an Italian barber?
One is a raving showman and the other is a shaving Roman.

I went to the pet shop and asked for five bees. The pet shop owner counted the bees out onto the counter 1, 2, 3, 4, 5, 6. I said "there's six there" and he said "Don't worry, that's a free bee".

Did you hear about the man who refused to believe he had fallen in a river in Egypt?
He was in denial.

A man goes to a fancy dress party as a tortoise with a woman strapped on his back, he's asked "why have you got a woman strapped to your back?" and he says "that's Michelle".

What do you call a place where they make things that are just OK?
A satis-factory.

Why can't you trust atoms?
Because they literally make up everything.

A child says to his dad "Where does poo come from?" The dad says "you eat food, it goes through your stomach and comes out the other end" so the child says "Well where does Tigger come from then?"

Did you hear about the Frenchman who could only count to seven?
He had a huit allergy.

What football team do witches support?
West Broom.

How do you get five donkeys into a fire engine?
Two in the front, two in the back and one on the top going eeyore, eeyore.

What is a pirate's favourite cheese?
Cheddarrrrrr.

Why did the fish blush?
Because it saw the ocean's bottom.

Why are turkeys so brave?
Because they're not chicken.

How do you kill a circus?
Go for the juggler.

A friend of mine built a motorbike from wood. It has a wooden frame, wooden engine, wooden wheels and a wooden petrol tank. Did he ride it?
No, it wooden start.

Why was the broom late for work?
It overswept.

What type of shoes do spies wear?
Sneakers.

What happened to the dog that swallowed a firefly?
He barked with delight.

What did one pencil say to the other pencil?
You look sharp.

Why did the actor fall through the floorboards?
They were going through a stage.

What did the duck say after she bought a lip balm?
Put it on my bill.

Which is faster, hot or cold?
Hot, you can easily catch a cold.

What's worse than finding a worm in your apple?
Finding half a worm.

What happened when Bluebeard fell overboard in the Red Sea?
He got marooned.

What did one volcano say to the other volcano?
I lava you.

What animal is always at a baseball game?
A bat.

What happened when the world's tongue twister champion got arrested?
They gave him a long sentence.

What did the mum cow say to her calf?
It's pasture bedtime.

What did one plate say to the other?
Dinner is on me.

Why do Hummingbirds hum?
Because they don't know the words.

What do sprinters eat before a race?
Nothing, they fast.

What kind of cat likes living in water?
An octo-puss.

Why did the pony get sent to his room?
Because he wouldn't stop horsing around.

How do you stop a bull from charging?
Take away its bank card.

Why can't a leopard hide?
Because it is always spotted.

How do you get a squirrel to like you?
Act like a nut.

How do young bees get to school?
On the school buzz.

What is a tornado's favourite game to play?
Twister.

Why is a snake difficult to fool?
Because you can't pull its leg.

How do you talk to a giant?
You have to use big words.

What do you get when you cross a snail with a hedgehog?
A slowpoke.

What did the dog say when it sat on sandpaper?
Ruff!

How does the moon cut its hair?
Eclipse it.

Why do you go to bed every night?
Because the bed can't come to you.

What is the centre of gravity?
V.

Why did the belt go to prison?
It held someone's pants up.

A man went into a pet shop and asked to buy a goldfish, the shop owner said "would you like an aquarium?" The man replied "I don't care what star sign it is"

What did the left eye say to the right eye?
Between you and I, something smells.

Two sausages are in a frying pan and one says to the other "cor… it's hot in here" and the other one says "aaahhhhh a talking sausage!".

What is the fastest thing in the canal?
A motorpike and sidecarp.

What did 0 say to 8?
Nice belt!

Which side of a cat is the furriest?
The outside.

Why did the toilet paper roll down the hill?
To get to the bottom.

What is a frog's favourite genre of music?
Hip hop.

How long does it take to brush a small dog?
Chihuahuas.

What was Postman Pat's favourite herb?
Parcel-y

What do you give someone with two left feet?
A pair of flip-flips.

What musical instrument can you find in the bathroom?
A tuba toothpaste.

Why can't you hear a pterodactyl go to the toilet?
Because the "p" is silent.

Where do fish keep their money?
In riverbanks.

Where do ships go when they are sick?
To the dock.

Why didn't the skeleton go to the party?
Because she had nobody to go with.

Breaking News - Scientists have discovered what is believed to be the world's largest bed sheet, more on this story as it unfolds

A wife texts her husband on a cold winter morning and says "Windows frozen, won't open."
He texts back saying "pour some lukewarm water on it and hit the edges gently with a hammer."
10 minutes later she texts back and says "the computer won't work at all now"

My mum asked if she could have a bit of peace and quiet while she was cooking tea…so I asked my Dad to take the batteries out of the smoke alarm.

I told a friend that my mum had set fire to all of her unpaid bills. They asked what her name is and I said "Bernadette"

Why should you never trust a snowman?
Because they're always up to snow good.

Why did the fly fly?
Because the spider spied her.

I heard a posh lady say to a man standing near her "How dare you break wind in front of me!" He replied "sorry I didn't know it was your turn".

I went to my doctor today and he told me my sugar levels were too high so when I got home I moved my sugar bowl to a lower shelf.

A bear walks into a bar and says "Can I have a pint of beer and ………………………………… a bag of nuts?" And the barman says "Sure, but why the big paws?"

What wobbles and flies?
A jellycopter

What does a vampire never eat for lunch?
A steak sandwich.

A man went into a chip shop with a cod under his arm and said to the woman behind the counter "Do you sell fishcakes?" and the woman behind the counter said "No, sorry we don't" and the man said "that's a shame" pointing to the cod under his arm "it's his birthday tomorrow."

A man stopped me in town and asked where he could find Pets At Home?
I suggested he looked under his sofa.

Where do you find giant snails?
At the end of a giant's fingers.

A man went to the doctors and said "I think I'm suffering with hearing loss" The Doctor said "Can you describe the symptoms?" The man said "of course I can, Homer is a bald guy and Marge has big blue hair.

I took the shell off my racing snail as I thought it would make him faster. If anything though it just made him more sluggish.

A man walks into a chip shop and asks for fish and chips twice please. The woman behind the counter says - I heard you the first time!

What is a foot long and slippery?
A slipper.

When is an Australian bear not a bear?
When it does not have the koalafications.

Knock, knock. Who's there? A librarian. A libra-shhuusshh

How do you make a Swiss roll?
Push him down a hill.

How do you make a Venetian blind?
Poke him in the eyes.

How do you make a Maltese cross?
Kick him in the shins.

What did one toilet say to the other toilet?
You look a bit flushed.

Why do the French eat snails?
Because they don't like fast food.

Why are dogs terrible dancers?
Because they have two left feet.

What type of snakes do you find on cars?
Windscreen Vipers.

Why was Cinderella such a poor football player?
Because her coach was a pumpkin.

Name a hungry horse in four letters.
MTGG.

How do you comfort an English teacher?
There, their, they're.

Where do pencils go on their holidays?
Pencil-vania.

What did baby corn say to mummy corn?
"Where's popcorn?"

What is a frog's favourite drink?
Croak-a-cola.

What do Ninjas eat for lunch?
Kung-food.

How do snails keep their shells shiny?
They use snail varnish.

Why do birds fly South in the winter?
Because it's too far to walk.

How do cows do their sums?
With a cow-culator.

What do cats like for breakfast?
Mice crispies.

What did the water say to the boat?
Nothing, it just waved.

Why are fish so intelligent?
Because they are always in schools.

What do you get from a pampered cow?
Spoiled milk.

What lies at the bottom of the ocean and twitches?
A nervous wreck.

Why do scuba divers fall backwards into the water?
Because if they fell forwards they'd fall into the boat.

Why would you invite a mushroom to a birthday party?
Because he's a fun-guy.

What is the difference between roast beef and pea soup?
Anyone can roast beef…

Why did the chicken go to the gym?
Because he was working on his pecks.

Vincent Van Gough walks into a bar and the bar person offers him a drink…"No thank you" said Vincent, "I've got one 'ere".

Why do calculators make the best friends?
Because you can count on them.

Where do aliens go to get drunk?
To a Mars bar.

Why did the scientist install a knocker on her door?
She wanted to win the No-bell prize.

Why do giraffes have long necks?
Because their feet smell.

"I'm really annoyed with my dog, he'll chase anyone on a bicycle". "So what are you going to do? Leave him at the dog's home? Give him away? Sell him?" "No, nothing that drastic. I think I'll just take his bike off him".

Where do rabbits go after they marry?
On their bunnymoon.

What kind of lion doesn't roar?
A dandelion.

How do you stop an astronaut's baby crying?
You rocket.

What's the difference between people from Dubai and Abu Dhabi?
People from Dubai don't like the Flintstones but people from Abu Dhabi do!

What goes "Oh oh oh?"
Father Christmas walking backwards.

How does a spud farmer guarantee that he will be able to do a full day of work?
He gets up potato clock.

Patient - I need a doctor's appointment.
Receptionist - OK - how about 10 tomorrow?
Patient - No I don't need that many.

What is the smartest insect?
A Spelling Bee.

Police officer - I am sorry to tell you that your son set the school on fire.
Parents - Was it arson?
Police officer - Yes it was your son.

What is a pirate's favourite letter?
It be the C.

What type of dog would you find on a toilet?
A poo-dle.

Son - What is that lion and witch doing in your wardrobe, Dad?
Dad - It's Narnia business!

What did the llama say when she got kicked out of the zoo?
"Alpaca my bags!"

What kind of dog did Dracula have?
A bloodhound.

Doctor, doctor, I feel like a pair of curtains. Well pull yourself together.

Knock, knock. Who's there? Arch. Arch who? Bless you.

Knock, knock. Who's there? Yoda lady. Yoda lady who? I didn't know you could sing!

What's the difference between ignorance and apathy?
I don't know and I don't care.

What goes ha ha ha ha thud?
Someone laughing their head off.

What happens if you swallow Christmas decorations?
You get tinselitis.

What do cats like eating in the summer?
Mice cream cones.

Wife - What is the difference between a postbox and a parrot?
Husband - I don't know.
Wife - Well I won't ask you to post a letter for me then!

What's the difference between sprouts and bogeys?
Kids won't eat sprouts.

Where do sheep go to get their hair cut?
The baa-baa shop.

What is a snake's favourite subject?
Hiss-tory.

What's red and bad for your teeth?
A brick.

How do trees get on the internet?
They log on.

Why didn't the teddy bear want pudding?
Because he was stuffed.

What has one wheel and flies?
A wheelbarrow full of horse manure.

What do you get if you jiggle a cow?
A milkshake.

Why did the chicken cross the playground?
To get to the other slide.

What do snowmen call their kids?
Chill-dren.

Why did the lion eat the tightrope walker?
Because he wanted a well-balanced meal.

What kind of tree fits in your hand?
A palm tree.

When do monkeys fall from the sky?
During Ape-ril showers.

Where do sheep spend their summer holidays?
The Baaaaa-hamas.

What is a cat's favourite pudding?
Chocolate mouse.

What fish swims at night?
A starfish.

How do you drown a Hipster?
In the mainstream.

What does a clock do when it's hungry?
It goes back for seconds.

What did one hat say to another?
You wait here, I'll go on ahead.

How do you stay warm in any room?
Go to the corner, it's always 90 degrees.

How did the scientist freshen her breath?
With experi-mints.

Why do bees have sticky hair?
Because they use a honeycomb.

How do you make a tissue dance?
Put a little boogie in it.

What tables don't require any maths?
Dinner tables.

My daughter asked me "Mum, can you do my maths homework for me?" I said "No love, it wouldn't be right". She sighed…"Well at least you could try".

What did one DNA strand say to the other DNA strand? Does my bum look big in these genes?

Why should you never argue with a 90-degree angle? Because they are always right.

I said to my friend: "I saw an octopus rob a bank this morning!" She said "Did it have a gun?" I said "No, but it was well armed".

Why did Mickey Mouse go up to space?
He wanted to find Pluto.

Why do dogs like mobile phones?
Because they have collar ID.

I lost two fingers on one hand, so I asked my doctor if I would still be able to write with it. She said, "Maybe, but I wouldn't count on it."

I told my doctor that I could hear a constant buzzing noise. She said, "Don't worry, it's just a bug going round."

What kind of award did the dentist receive?
A little plaque.

What type of snake ate all the desserts?
A Pie-thon.

What is a frog's favourite game?
Leap frog.

Why couldn't the duck stop laughing?
He was quacking up.

Why are sports stadiums always so cold?
Because they are filled with fans.

What did the mummy flower say to the baby flower?
Hi, bud.

What are ten things you can always count on?
Your fingers.

What did the triangle say to the circle?
You're pointless.

Which King loved fractions?
Henry the 8th.

How do polar bears make their beds?
With sheets of ice and blankets of snow.

What did one wall say to the other wall?
I'll meet you at the corner.

What do you get on every birthday?
A year older.

How many apples grow on a tree?
All of them.

Knock, knock. Who's there? Cows go. Cows go who?
No, cows go Moo!

Why are ghosts bad liars?
Because you can see straight through them.

Why did the man run around his bed?
Because he was trying to catch up on his sleep.

Why shouldn't you bother talking to circles?
Because there's no point.

What do librarians take when they go fishing?
Book worms.

Why did the man put sugar on his pillow?
He wanted to have sweet dreams.

Can a kangaroo jump higher than the Empire State Building?
Of course, the Empire State Building can't jump.

What do fish play on the piano?
Scales.

What kind of music do balloons hate?
Pop!

Why are elephants so wrinkled?
Because they take too long to iron.

Why did the teacher put on sunglasses?
Because her pupils were so bright.

What kind of room doesn't have doors?
A mushroom.

What's a really sad strawberry called?
A blueberry.

What did the Dalmatian say after eating a huge meal?
That hit the spot.

What do lawyers wear when they go to court?
Law-suits.

What's the most expensive fish?
A goldfish.

What do Alexander the Great and Winnie the Pooh have in common?
Their middle name.

What's the best way to throw a birthday party on Mars?
You planet.

Why should you never trust a pig with your biggest secret?
Because it's bound to squeal.

Why did the boy throw his clock from his bedroom window?
Because he wanted to see time fly.

What time is it when a lion walks into a room?
Time to leave!

Where should you go if you want to learn how to make ice cream?
Sundae school.

What kind of jobs do funny chickens have?
They are comedi-hens.

Why did the Oreo go to the dentist?
Because her filling fell out.

Which hand is better to write with?
Neither, it's better to write with a pencil.

Why do all witches wear black?
So you can't tell which witch is which.

What type of shoes do frogs have lots of pairs of?
Open-toad sandals.

How did Darth Vader know what Luke had bought him for Christmas?
He felt his presents.

What did Venus say to Saturn?
Give me a ring sometime.

What do you give a hurt lemon?
Lemon aid.

Why did the nurse take a red pen to work?
In case she needed to draw blood.

Why did the melon jump in the lake?
Because it wanted to be a watermelon.

What is the most famous type of animal in the sea?
A starfish.

What kind of fruit do twins like the best?
Pears.

I try not to tell Dad jokes. But when I do he finds them funny.

What's the strongest type of sea creature?
Mussels.

What sweet treat is always last to arrive?
Choco-late.

Why do ducks have feathers on their tails?
To cover their butt quacks.

Why don't lamps ever sink when they're in water?
Because they're light.

What did the T-Rex say to the Velociraptor?
Nothing, they're extinct.

What type of dog is good at telling the time?
A watch-dog.

What room does a ghost not need?
A living room.

Why did the puppy always get top marks at school?
He was the teacher's pet.

Which planet is the best singer?
Nep-tune.

What sound do porcupines make when they kiss?
Ouch!

What did the firefly say to her BFF?
You glow girl.

How did the pirate get his flag so cheaply?
He bought it on sail.

Why did the snake cross the road?
To get to the other sssside.

Where do spiders play their football matches?
Webley Stadium.

Why did the old man fall in the well?
Because he couldn't see that well.

Why do barbers make good drivers?
Because they know a lot of shortcuts.

Two men meet on opposite sides of a river. One shouts to the other "I need you to help me get to the other side" the other man shouts back "You're already on the other side".

What do you call a fish wearing a bow tie?
Sofishticated.

The teacher said "If I had eight oranges in one hand and eleven oranges in the other hand what would I have?"
Heidi replied "You'd have massive hands".

How are false teeth like stars?
They come out at night.

A tortoise got attacked by three snails. He was asked for a description of the suspects and he replied "I don't know, it all happened so quick".

What do you say to a rabbit on her birthday?
Hoppy Birthday!

Why was the equal sign so humble?
Because he wasn't greater than or less than anyone else.

Why don't pirates shower before they walk the plank?
Because they'll just wash up on the shore later.

What's brown, hairy and wears sunglasses?
A coconut on his holidays.

Why are cats good at video games?
Because they have nine lives.

What fruit do scarecrows love the most?
Straw-berries.

What key opens a banana?
A mon-key.

Are black cats bad luck?
Yes, if you're a mouse.

What do you call two witches living together?
Broommates.

What is a vampire's favourite fruit?
A blood orange.

Where do baby ghosts go during the day?
Day-scare centres.

How does a sheep say Merry Christmas?
Fleece Navidad.

How can you tell which rabbits are the oldest in a group?
Just look for the grey hares.

Why did the robber jump in the shower?
He wanted to make a clean getaway.

WHAT DO YOU CALL A...

What do you call a girl who is hard to find? Heidi.

What do you call an ant who fights crime? A vigilante.

What do you call a man with a plank of wood on his head?
Edward.

What do you call a man with three planks of wood on his head?
Edward Woodward.

What do you call a man with a spade on his head?
Doug.

What do you call a man without a spade on his head?
Douglas.

What do you call a teacher who is always late?
Mister Bus.

What do you call a man with a seagull on his head?
Cliff.

What do you call a man with a pile of leaves on his head?
Russell.

What do you call a man with a car on his head?
Jack.

What do you call a snake on a building site?
A Boa Constructor.

What do you call a woman with one leg longer than the other?
Eileen.

What do you call a dinosaur fart?
A blast from the past.

What do you call a man floating in the sea?
Bob.

What do you call somebody with no body and no nose?
Nobody knows.

What do you call a fly with no wings?
A walk.

What do you call a blind dinosaur?
Doyouthinkhesawus.

What do you call a blind dinosaur's dog?
Doyouthinkhesawusrex.

What do you call a magic dog?
A labracadabrador.

What do you call an M&M that went to university?
A smartie.

What do you call a cow that plays the trumpet?
A moo-sician.

What do you call a train full of toffees?
A chew chew train.

What do you call a broken pencil?
Pointless.

What do you call a man with no pants on?
Nicholas.

What do you call a duck that gets all A's?
A wise quaker.

What do you call a penguin outside Buckingham Palace?
Lost.

What do you call the lights on Noah's Ark?
Flood lights.

What do you call a droid that takes the long way around?
R2 detour.

What do you call a fake spaghetti?
An impasta.

What do you call a ghost's true love?
His ghoul-friend.

What do you call a man with no shins?
Tony.

What do you call a crate of ducks?
A box of quackers.

What do you call an elephant that doesn't matter?
An Irrelephant.

What do you call just married spiders?
Newly webs.

What do you call people who are afraid of Santa Claus?
Claustrophobic.

What do you call a man with a pole through his leg?
Rodney.

What do you call a girl who stands inside the goalposts and stops the ball rolling away?
Anette.

What do you call a line of men waiting for their haircuts?
A barbe-queue.

What do you call an exploding monkey?
A babooooom!

What do you call two birds in love?
Tweethearts.

What do you call a dinosaur with an extensive vocabulary?
A thesaurus.

What do you call James Bond having a bath?
Bubble 07.

What do you call a man with a rubber toe?
Roberto.

What do you call a camel with three humps?
Humphrey.

What do you call a bagel that can fly?
A plain bagel.

What do you call a pig who knows karate?
A pork chop.

What do you call a skunk who flies a helicopter?
A smelly-copter pilot.

What do you call backbirds that stick together?
Vel-crows.

What do you call a sleeping bull?
A bull-dozer.

What do you call a tiny mother?
A minimum.

What do you call a boomerang that doesn't come back?
A stick.

ONE LINERS...

My wife is on a tropical food diet, the house is full of the stuff, it's enough to make a mango crazy.

My wife asked me if I had seen the dog bowl. I answered, "To be honest, I didn't even know he played cricket."

Yesterday I won a year's supply of Marmite...one jar.

I sold my Hoover the other day because it was just in the corner gathering dust.

I've just opened a new restaurant called Karma. There's no menu, we just give you what you deserve.

A lorry load of tortoises crashed into a train load of terrapins, what a turtle disaster!

I'll tell you what I love doing more than anything and that's trying to pack myself into a small suitcase, I can hardly contain myself.

The other day my wife asked me to pass her her lipstick, I accidentally passed her a glue stick. She's still not talking to me.

The other day I sent my girlfriend a huge pile of snow, I rang her up and I said "Did you get my drift?"

My father used to work in the circus as a stilt walker. When I was a child I always looked up to him.

Do you know what's odd? Every other number.

A tin of alphabetti spaghetti spilled on the floor in the supermarket today…it could have spelled disaster.

My friend thinks he is smart. He said that the only food that can make him cry is an onion, so I threw a coconut at him.

People are always telling me to live my dreams. But I don't want to be naked in an exam that I haven't revised for!

My four year old son has been learning Spanish, but he can only say the word please. That's poor for four.

It is lunch time, so for my next trick I will eat a musical instrument sandwich…drum roll please.

I managed to burn my Hawaiian pizza, I should have used aloha temperature.

I recently got squished by a lot of my books. I only have my shelf to blame.

Two goldfish in a tank, one says to the other "How do you start this thing?"

I find sleeping really easy. In fact I can do it with my eyes closed.

I saw this bloke going up a hill with a wheelbarrow full of horseshoes, four leaf clovers and rabbit's feet. I thought, "He's pushing his luck."

I hate Russian dolls, they're so full of themselves.

I've just got back from the hospital...the doctor thinks I might have pneumonoultramicroscopicsilicoconiosis, but it's hard to say.

I have had to quit my job at the cat rescue shelter. They reduced meowers.

I wrote a song about a tortilla, well actually, it's more of a rap.

Did you hear about the kidnapping at school? It's ok. He woke up.

I walked into a bar last night. Broke three ribs. It was an iron bar!

My Dad invented a cold air balloon, but it never really took off.

I tried to sue the airport for misplacing my luggage. I lost my case.

A kid threw a lump of cheddar at me. I thought "That's not very mature".

I've just started at the gym and my personal trainer asked "are you flexible?" I said "yes, I can do any day of the week".

I've just failed my abseiling exam, I let myself down badly.

I cleaned the attic with the wife the other day…she still can't get the cobwebs out of her hair.

I have a new job as a bell ringer. On my first day I hope that they will be showing me the ropes.

The inventor of the ballet skirt was struggling with a name for it. Finally he put tu and tu together.

I accidentally got tomato ketchup in my eyes. Now I have heinzsight.

Did you hear about the hen who counts her own eggs? She is a mathemachicken.

Never trust maths teachers who use graph paper. They're always plotting something.

Long fairy tales have a tendency to dragon.

To whoever stole my copy of Microsoft office I will find you. You have my word.

I was warned about starting my own skiing company, apparently it's a slippery slope.

My wife fainted onto the baggage carousel at the airport but thankfully she came around.

I applied for a job polishing mirrors, it's something I can see myself doing.

I learned everything I know about trapeze online, I couldn't have done it without the net.

Five ants rented a house then five more ants moved in, now they are ten-ants.

I couldn't understand why the frisbee kept getting bigger and then it hit me.

A man went to the doctors with a strawberry on his nose, the doctor said "I've got some cream for that".

I love telling people about the benefits of eating dried grapes. It is all about raisin awareness.

A man came running at me with a guitar about to hit me. I said "Is that a fret?"

I only know 25 letters of the alphabet. I don't know why.

I can't believe I got sacked from the calendar factory. All I did was take one day off.

I walked into the bar the other day and ordered a double…the barman brought out a bloke who looked just like me.

During a short train journey across London I taught my little dog to play the trumpet, within sixty minutes we went from Barking to Tooting.

You can't get mad at lazy people, they've never done anything.

I make my French omelettes with just one egg because one egg is unoeuf.

Two cows in a field, one says "Moo" and the other says "hey, I was just about to say that".

I never thought I'd be the type of person who'd get up early in the morning to exercise…I was right.

I tried to climb that really tall tower in France but Eiffel off.

Just saw a box of After Eights for sale on Ebay…mint condition.

I hated my job as an origami teacher, too much paperwork.

As a painter I'm proud to say that some of my work is on show in the National Gallery…I did the skirting boards.

I was awake all night worrying about where the sun had gone...and then it dawned on me.

I don't want to brag but I finished a jigsaw in under a week and it said 2 to 4 years on the box.

I love pressing F5, it's so refreshing.

I don't like puns about air conditioners...not a fan.

I ate a clock yesterday...it was very time consuming.

Would a cardboard belt be a waist of paper?

I was going to tell a pizza joke but it was too cheesy.

I just heard that two slices of bread got married. Apparently the ceremony was wonderful. Well that was until someone decided to toast the bride and groom.

I was wondering why a lot of people were signing up for Anger Management classes, but it seems it's all the rage.

I'm trying to organise a hide and seek tournament but it's really hard to find good players.

I have got a job in a salt and pepper factory - it's just seasonal work.

My mate keeps racing pigeons - he never wins!

I tried water polo, but my horse drowned.

I once did a tandem parachute jump, it was amazing, but sadly the bike was a write off.

Tennis ball machine for sale £100, I've had it over a year now and it's served me well.

If at first you don't succeed then skydiving isn't for you.

If the sign says road works then why are they fixing it?

The quietest place I ever lived was next door to a bowling alley. It was so quiet that you could hear a pin drop.

I paid £30 for a belt that didn't fit. Huge waist.

The joke I regret the most is about a boomerang and a ghost…it still comes back to haunt me.

Someone stole my mood ring. I'm not sure how I feel about that.

A dung beetle walks into a bar and says "Excuse me, is this stool taken?"

She sells seashells by the seashore, surely that's the worst place to sell them?

Before the crow bar was invented crows had to drink at home.

Sometimes I tuck my knees into my chest and lean forward. That's just how I roll.

A man was found guilty of over using commas. The judge warned him to expect a really long sentence.

My wife just found out that I replaced our bed with a trampoline. She hit the roof.

My Dad has the heart of a lion…and a lifetime ban from the zoo.

Today a man knocked on my door and asked for a small donation towards the local swimming pool. I gave him a glass of water.

Velcro…what a rip off.

My wife and I often laugh about how competitive we are, but I laugh louder.

I was following a magic tractor down a country lane. I knew it was magic when it turned into a field.

Don't spell part backwards, it's a trap.

I used to run a dating service for chickens, I had to close it as I was struggling to make hens meet.

A lorry load of Marmite has crashed on the M4 today. The police say to avoid the yeast bound carriageway.

I've decided to follow in my father's footsteps and become a clown. I've got big shoes to fill.

If you need help building an ark, I Noah guy.

I just flew into the country. My arms are so tired.

I failed my maths exam so many times at school I can't even count.

One of my cows didn't produce any milk today. It was an udder failure.

Local authorities are investigating an illegal theatre production where the cast is entirely made up of chickens. Police suspect fowl play.

Don't you just hate it when someone answers their own questions? I do.

Two artists had an art contest. It ended in a draw.

You'll never guess who I bumped into on the way to the opticians? Everyone.

My friend asked me to round up his 37 sheep and I said 40.

I slept like a log last night…woke up in the fireplace.

CELEBRITY JOKES...

TV royalty Lorraine Kelly - A group of cannibals put a clown in their cooking pot, they gave it a stir, let it simmer and then asked each other "Does this taste funny to you?"

Former Blue Peter presenter Sarah Greene - Where do you find a tortoise with no legs? Where you left him.

Dogs behaving very badly presenter Graeme Hall - Dog owner: My dog has no nose. Friend: OMG! How does he smell? Dog owner: Terrible.

Designer and Claireabella business owner Claire Barratt: - Why did the orange go to the doctors? Because it wasn't peeling very well.

Horrid Henry The Movie's Dick and Dom - What's invisible and smells like bananas? Monkey farts.

The most common similarity between a fish and a baby is the inability to use heavy machinery.

There was an old man from Ocket,
Who went for a ride in a rocket.
The rocket went bang, his ears went twang.
And he found his nose in his pocket.

Comedian Arthur Smith - A woman goes to the doctor and says I can't say my "th's" or "f's". The doctors says "well you can't say fairer than that then".

Poet Ian McMillan - What did the Yorkshireman do when he ran out of sellotape?
He buy gum.

Ex Premier league referee Jeff Winter - I saw a bloke walking round the supermarket shouting "Cauliflower, broccoli, cauliflower, broccoli!" He must have had florets.

Newsreader Faye Barker - What's brown and sticky?
A stick.

West End actor Dan Buckley: - A skeleton walks into a bar and asks for a pint of beer and a mop.

Ex professional footballer Peter Reid - My wife told me to stop impersonating a flamingo. I had to put my foot down.

Newsreader Alyx Barker - A police officer caught two burglars, one had a sack full of stolen batteries, the other with a stash of stolen fireworks. He charged one and let the other one off.

Novelist Gina Kirkham - I was in a shoe shop trying on a shoe. I said "It's too tight" And the assistant said "Try it with the tongue out." I said "It'th nho ghood, it'th thtill thoo thight."

Caversham United FC - What do you call a goat dressed up as a clown?
A silly Billy.

Comedian Darren Walsh - I tried to get in to a fundraising event, but I got Heidi'ed

BBC sport presenter Giulia Bould - What do you get if you cross a vampire with a snowman?
Frostbite.

Novelist Freya North - What do you do when your nose goes on strike? Pick it.

Comedian Kate Robbins - I've made a ventriloquist dummy out of some old carpet…it's ruggish.

Comedy writer Mike Fenton Stevens - Last week I replaced every window in my house and then I discovered I had a crack in my glasses.

Lidl supermarket - Why did the skeleton burp?
Because he didn't have the guts to trump.

Capital Radio DJ Aimee Vivian - What do you call cheese that isn't yours?
Nacho cheese.

Bronte, contestant on the 2024 series of Gladiators - When is a fire door not a fire door?
When it's ajar.

Nia, contestant on the 2024 series of Gladiators - Why did the bike fall over?
Because it was two tired.

BBC North West Tonight presenter Steve Saul - People often ask me how I smuggle food into the cinema...well I have a few Twix up my sleeve.

TV presenter Fern Britton - Where do police officers live?
999 Letsby Avenue.

Comedy writer Paul Kerensa - Why didn't the pony speak?
He was a little horse.

Rugby League TV presenter Ross Fiddes - How do you tell the difference between a cow and a bull?
It's either one or the udder.

Actress Helen Lederer - Why did the golfer wear two pairs of trousers?
In case he got a hole in one.

Novelist Cara Hunter - A man goes into a pet shop and says "Can I buy a wasp?". The shop owner says "We don't tell wasps." The man says "But you had one in the window yesterday."

Olympian athlete, Katharine Merry - Why did the banana go to the doctor? Because he wasn't peeling very well.

54

Former Everton and Wales goalkeeper Neville Southall - What do you call a man with a seagull on his head? Cliff

CBeebies and CBBC presenter Evie Pickerill - What did the cheese say to himself in the mirror? Hallou-mi!

Heidi's favourite Gladiator Fire! - Knock, knock. Who's there? Heidi. Heidi who? Heidi-clare war on you.

The Chase's Menace, Darragh Ennis - Two men were sentenced in court today for stealing a calendar, they got six months each.

X Factor second runner up in 2008, Eoghan Quigg - Why was Cinderella so bad at football? Because she kept running away from the ball.

TV presenter Alison Hammond - Why didn't the skeleton go to the party? Because he had nobody to go with.

R I D D L E S ...

1) It belongs to you but your friends use it more, what is it?

2) Feed me and I live, give me a drink and I die, what am I?

3) What is as light as a feather but no person can hold it for long?

4) How many letters are in the alphabet?

5) I am full of holes but strong as steel. What am I?

6) You can see me in water but I never get wet. What am I?

7) Before Mount Everest was discovered, what was the highest mountain in the world?

8) What invention lets you look right through a wall?

9) A bus driver goes the wrong way down a one way street. He goes straight past uniformed police officers who are on duty and they don't stop him. Why?

10) What question can you never honestly answer yes to?

11) A tree doubles in height each year until it reaches its full height after ten years. How many years did it take it to reach half its full height?

12) A man is pushing his car along the road and comes to a hotel. He shouts "I'm bankrupt!"
Why?

13) I make a loud voice when I am changing. When I do change I get bigger, but weigh less.
What am I?

14) Which came first, the egg or the chicken?

15) A group of 10 friends are going out for pizza, but only two of them have an umbrella to keep them dry. They all manage to walk all the way to the pizza place without any of them getting wet. How?

16) What has only got two words, but thousands of letters?

17) A girl is in the middle of a flat field alone. She kicks a ball 10 feet away and it comes straight back to her. How?

18) Who can finish a book without finishing a sentence?

19) Alex is the father of Sam, but Sam is not the son of Alex. How?

20) What has a head and a tail but no body?

21) How far can you walk into the woods?

22) What has a tongue but can't speak?

23) What type of bed can't you sleep in?

24) What has four legs but can't walk?

25) What has teeth but can't bite?

26) An English word has 5 letters but if you take away 4 of the letters it is still pronounced the same. What is the word?

27) When you do not know what I am then I am something. But when you know what I am then I am nothing. What am I?

28) How many months have 28 days in them?

29) What has to be broken before you can use it?

30) There is a bungalow in which everything is yellow. Yellow walls, yellow doors and yellow furniture. What colour are the stairs?

31) What gets bigger the more you take from it?

32) It goes uphill and downhill but it doesn't move, what is it?

33) How do you spell candy using only two letters?

34) What goes up but never comes down?

35) What has got a bottom at the top?

36) What can you put in a bucket of water to make it lighter?

37) The more you take the more you leave behind. What am I?

38) What goes up but never comes down?

39) Can you name three consecutive days without mentioning Monday, Thursday or Saturday?

40) Imagine you are in a dark room. How do you get out?

41) I never ask any questions but I am always answered. What am I?

42) What tastes better than it smells?

43) Say my name and I disappear. What am I?

44) What has a forest but no tree, cities but no people and rivers but no water?

45) What can you hold in your right hand but never in your left hand?

46) I am tall when I'm young and short when I'm old. What am I?

47) What type of dress can you never wear?

48) How did Steven marry three women in Cheshire without divorcing any of them, without legally separating from any of them and without any of them dying?

49) Two girls were born to the same mother, on the same day, at the same time, in the same month and year but they are not twins. How can this be?

50) What has a neck but no head and two arms but no hands?

Answers on pages 69 and 70

FRIEND'S JOKES...

Lillie Jones - What type of pants do clouds wear? Thunderpants.

Josh - Why are maths books always upset? Because they have a lot of problems.

Ella Fergus - What time is it when an elephant sits on your fence? Time to get a new fence.

Seve. J. - What is a penguin's favourite family member? Aunt Arctica.

Elodie Murray - What do you get if you cross fish with elephants? Swimming trunks.

Katie Perks - Knock, knock. Who's there? I did ap. I did ap who? Eurgh, too much information!

Ellie-May Davies - What do you call a huge pile of cats? A meow-ntain!

Darci Needham- Doctor Doctor I think I'm a clock, well I think you are too wound up.

Frankie Needham - Knock knock, who's there? An interrupting cow. An interrupt — MOO!

Apollo Misbah - Why did the golfer wear two pairs of trousers? In case he got a hole in one!

Miss Woodland - Why did the cow cross the road? To go to the mooooovies.

Isabelle. H. - Why couldn't the pony sing a lullaby? She was a little horse.

Darcey. G. - What does a cloud wear under his raincoat? Thunderwear.

Ollie - Knock knock. Who's there? Cows go. Cows go who? No cows go Moo silly.

Jess. C. - My dog has no nose. How does it smell? Terrible.

Erin. G. - Why was the mouse's home so tidy? Because it was squeaky clean.

Yunus. G, Charlie Price and Aiden. C. - Knock knock, Who's there? Europe. Europe who? I'm not a poo, you are!

Alfie. G. - Why did the chicken cross the road? To get to the other side

Phoebe. O. - Knock knock. Who's there? The chicken. The chicken who? The chicken who just crossed the road.

Ashton - Why did the picture go to jail? Because he was framed.

Zach. W. - What part of the solar system is named after a body part? Uranus.

Clara. S. - Why did the toilet paper roll down the hill? To get to the bottom.

Imogen - What do you call a bear with no teeth? A gummy bear.

Ava - Knock Knock, who's there? Robin, Robin who? Robin de bank.

Archie. B. - Why do seagulls fly over the sea? Because if they flew over the bay they'd be bagels.

Jacob. D. - Why was six afraid of seven? Because seven eight nine.

Lily Freeman. - What do you call a puppy with a fever - a hot dog.

Selimhan. H. - Knock knock, who's there? Howarr yeh - Howarr yeh who? - I am good thanks, how are you?

Tommy - What is invisible and smells like carrots? Bunny farts

Woody - Why was the sand wet? Because the sea weed.

Rex - What's brown and sticky? A stick. What's also brown and sticky? Your dad's poo.

Minnie - Why did the chicken cross the road? To buy deodorant because it stinks.

Denise - What is the most common owl in the UK? The teat.

Veronica Denson - What type of socks do polar bears wear? They don't, they have bear feet

Tommy age 7 - What did the drummer call his twin daughters? Anna One, Anna Two!

Emilia Wilson - What happens to a frog that is illegally parked? It gets toad.

Freya Wilson - Which is faster, hot or cold? Hot, because you can catch a cold.

Mark Strickland-Kehoe - What do you call a kangaroo wearing a sweater? A woolly jumper,

Pearl Cowley - Knock knock. Who's there? Ewan. Ewan who? No-one else, just me.

Martha Cowley - What does a polar bear eat for breakfast? Snowflakes with milk.

Andrew Cowley - What is a duck's favourite dip? Quackamole.

FUN FACTS...

The penguin which is called Eudyptula minor is the smallest penguin in the world at 33 cm's tall. However they have the highest velocity of poo and they can poop a distance greater than their height.

Tigers have striped skin, not just striped fur.

Australia is wider than the moon.

In Switzerland it is against the law to own only one guinea pig - they prefer company.

Each year at least 1 septillion snowflakes fall from the sky that is 1,000,000,000,000,000,000,000,000,000,000,000,000,000,000 (42 zeroes!)

In Singapore it is illegal to chew gum.

An Australian man won the lottery. He filmed an interview for the news where they asked him to re-enact buying a ticket…he did so and won again!

Octopuses have blue blood and nine brains.

The actors who did the voices for Minnie and Mickey Mouse got married in real life.

The UK consumes more baked beans than the rest of the world combined.

You cannot hum while holding your nose.

For 90% of people the distance from their wrist to their elbow will be the same length as their foot.

Venus is the only planet which spins clockwise.

Crocodiles are able to regrow their teeth many times over in their lifetime. The replacements grow inside the old tooth so that the tooth doesn't leave a gap when it falls out.

Hot water freezes quicker than cold water.

Donald Duck's middle name is Fauntleroy.

The pupils of a goat's eyes are rectangular.

Wombat poo is cube shaped.

When they're happy bunny's do a binky which is a jump and twist in the air.

Gallium is a metal and its melting point is so low that it would melt on a summer's day. Magicians use it to bend metal objects such as a teaspoon whilst pretending to use their minds but actually they are using the heat from their hands.

A bus powered by the gas from cow manure became the world's fastest bus in 2015 with speeds over 75 mph.

The Golden Gate Bridge in San Francisco, USA, hums and whistles in the wind thanks to the shape of the railings. The singing can be so loud that it can be heard nearly 3 miles away.

Inmates at a jail in Brazil had the chance to reduce their time in prison by pedalling exercise bikes that generated electricity for a local town.

The Guiness Book of world Records was originally created to settle bar bets.

Vatican City has its own national football team. There are only 900 people in the country so when Vatican City play over 1% of the whole population are on the football pitch!

It is believed that the umbrella sea slug has 750,000 teeth!

There is a restaurant in Taiwan that serves food in mini toilets. Drinks are served in mini-urinals. Pudding is chocolate ice cream and is served in a potty.

Michelin stars were created by the maker of tyres in order to get people to drive further to the best restaurants.

When you turn the tap on, hot and cold water sounds different. Hot water has a higher pitch and the human ear can tell the difference.

The gap between your eyebrows is called a glabella.

The smell after rainfall is called petrichor.

The plastic or metallic coating on the end of a shoelace is an aglet.

A wamble is the noise your tummy makes when it rumbles.

The prongs on a fork are called tines.

We often don't like/recognise the sound of our own voice and this can be because the bones in our head make our voice sound deeper to us.

The little plastic thing in your pizza box to hold the lid away from your pizza is called a box tent.

A jar of Nutella sells somewhere in the world every 2.5 seconds.

The day after tomorrow is called overmorrow.

An average yawn lasts for six seconds.

Noises in a song which don't have any meaning like "la, la, la" are called vocables.

Tomato ketchup was once sold as a medicine.

Human beings cannot lick the point of their elbow.

The expiry date on UK crisps is always a Saturday.

A question mark and exclamation mark used together (?!) is called an interrobang.

The dot over an "i" or a "j" is called a tittle.

It takes eight minutes and nineteen seconds for the light from the Sun to reach the Earth.

The feeling of being bloated after eating or drinking too much is called crapulence.

From Charlotte - Bernard Clemmens did the longest recorded fart which was timed at 2 minutes 42 seconds.

The number four is the only number with the same amount of letters as its value.

Comedy writer Sian Harries - You can't feel fear and curiosity at the same time. So if you're ever scared of something try being curious about it.

RIDDLE ANSWERS...

1) Your name.
2) Fire.
3) Your breath.
4) There are 11 letters in the words 'THE ALPHABET'
5) A chain.
6) A reflection.
7) Mount Everest (it just hadn't been discovered yet).
8) A window.
9) He was walking.
10) Are you sleeping?
11) 9 years. As it doubles in height each year and it's reached its maximum height at ten years, at 9 years it is half of its maximum height.
12) He is playing Monopoly.
13) Popcorn
14) The egg because Dinosaurs laid eggs before chickens were alive.
15) It isn't raining.
16) Post office.
17) She kicked the ball straight up in the air.
18) A prisoner in jail.
19) Sam is Alex's daughter.
20) A coin.
21) Half way, after that you are walking back out.
22) A shoe (by Heidi).
23) A riverbed.
24) A chair (or a table).
25) A comb (or a zip).

26) Queue (Q).
27) A riddle.
28) All of them.
29) An egg.
30) There are no stairs in a bungalow.
31) A hole.
32) A road.
33) C - AND - Y.
34) Your age.
35) A leg.
36) A hole.
37) Footsteps.
38) Your age.
39) Yesterday, today and tomorrow.
40) Stop imagining.
41) Mobile phone.
42) Your tongue.
43) Silence.
44) A map.
45) Your left hand.
46) A candle.
47) An address.
48) Steven is a vicar.
49) They also have a brother and are triplets.
50) A shirt.

DEDICATION

I dedicate this book to my Great Uncle Ian, my Mum and my Dad.

I also dedicate this book to my cousin Chris, because he's promised to dedicate his first book to me!

Thank you to my Mum and Dad for helping me write it.
Thank you to all my followers who have supported me along the way.
Thank you to James for designing the cover.
Thank you to everyone who gave me a joke, riddle or fact.
Thank you to the charity for always supporting me.
Thank you to everyone who donated money.
And finally a great big THANK YOU to everyone who bought this book, I hope you enjoy it and it makes you smile.

Printed in Great Britain
by Amazon